THIS BOOK BELONGS TO:

....

....

TORCHER
If found please return to:
DR. ERNEST DRAKE,
ST. LEONARD'S FOREST, HORSHAM.

CONTENTS

First published in the UK in 2005 by Templar Publishing,
an imprint of The Templar Company plc,
Pippbrook Mill, London Road, Dorking, Surrey RH4 1JE, UK.

Illustrations copyright © 2005 by Douglas Carrel.
Text and design copyright © 2005 by The Templar Company plc.
Designed by Jonathan Lambert & Nghiem Ta.
All Rights Reserved.
ISBN 1-84011-710-9
1 3 5 7 9 10 8 6 4 2
Manufactured in China.

PUBLISHER'S NOTE: This book purports to be the facsimile of an
original that was among the effects of Dr. Ernest Drake. It is possible
that he wrote it for a niece and nephew who needed a little more
information than was to be found in *Dragonology—the Complete Book of
Dragons*, said to have been originally published in 1895, and
republished by Templar Publishing in 2003.

templar publishing

www.dragonology.com

Dr. Ernest Drake's

Dragonology

Bringing up
Baby Dragons.

The Complete Guide.

Edited by

Dugald A. Steer, B.A. (Brist), S.A.S.D.

ILLUSTRATED.

THE TEMPLAR COMPANY:
PUBLISHERS OF RARE & UNUSUAL BOOKS.
[ALL RIGHTS RESERVED.]

"Few hobbies are quite so absorbing as
hatching and raising baby dragons."

AN INTRODUCTION TO DRAGON BREEDING.

There has been much talk of dragons recently, and a great deal of rummaging about in hedgerows, going on expeditions to remote mountain caves, exploring lost jungle cities, and setting off on trips to the icy wastes around the poles in search of them. At the *Secret and Ancient Society of Dragonologists* this has been a cause of some anxiety in case a dragon should fall into the hands of someone who lacked the knowledge and experience to care for it properly. Few hobbies are quite so absorbing as hatching and raising baby dragons, but there are not many that require such total care and dedication. It was with this in mind that I penned a new guide to dragon husbandry. And whether you choose to adopt an orphan dragon chick or hatch one from an egg, *Bringing Up Baby Dragons* will teach all you need to know about dragon care. From choosing the right breed and preparing a lair right up to the moment when you release your companion back into the wild, it will be a trusty guide.

Ernest Drake

FEATURES OF
DIFFERENT BREEDS.

When selecting the best breed of dragon to raise one must consider various factors: if one lives in a flat or house, if one has a garden, if one lives in town or in the country, how much exercise one can give the dragon, if there are children at home, and if one can keep it securely.

EUROPEAN *Draco occidentalis magnus*

DESPITE being the most popular dragon, the European dragon really does need a large, secure home with a considerable acreage of grounds, or at least a handy forest, if buildings are not to be torched willy-nilly, and friends and neighbours frightened, or worse.

*TORCHER
THE MIGHTY*

The charcoal brazier used to keep a european dragon's egg hot must be kept in a well-ventilated location.

KNUCKER *Draco troglodytes*

ONE of the few choices for those who live in a flat or apartment, the knucker is the smallest of all dragons. However, its tendency to eat anything when hungry means that it should not be kept where there are very young babies.

WEASEL

A knucker's egg may be kept warm on top of an ordinary stove.

FROST *Draco occidentalis maritimus*

RAISING a frost dragon from the egg is only really an option for those who live within the Arctic Circle. Frost chicks can tolerate warm temperatures, but staying above freezing for too long tends to make them sluggish, so the use of heating at home is not recommended.

SPITZ

A frost dragon's egg must be kept as cold as possible. An arrangement of a fan and a block of ice can help.

ASIAN *LUNG*

LUNG WEI

Draco orientalis magnus

THE proximity of running water is essential to the raising of *lung* chicks. Only attempt to raise them if you live near a stream, a waterfall or a suitable river.

Underwater breathing apparatus is required for tending lung *eggs.*

WYVERN *Draco africanus*

TO raise a wyvern chick, you must follow three rules: i. Exercise it a lot; ii. Give it plenty of walks; and iii. Take it to the park frequently. It doesn't tire easily.

SALAZAAR

A sturdy wheelbarrow will assist considerably in moving wyvern's eggs should the need ever arise. Be very careful not to drop the eggs onto your toes.

GUSANO

AMPHITHERE
Draco americanus mex

ONE of the more exotic breeds, an amphithere chick can be made to feel at home in a pyramid-shaped nest built of brick or stone. It loves humid conditions.

An amphithere's egg has a rubbery shell and it can be bounced without harming the embryo inside.

HOPPY

A high degree of variation in patterning on marsupial eggs help a mother dragon to identify her clutch.

MARSUPIAL _Draco marsupialis_

EASY to both hatch and raise, until the coming of man to Australia the marsupial dragon had no known natural enemies. Should a chick ever show signs of distress, the best remedy is to mimic its natural Blue Mountains environment by splashing a lot of eucalyptus oil about.

11

RARE AND EXOTIC BREEDS.

In addition to the common or garden varieties of dragon described on the previous pages, some breeders prefer to specialise in the raising of rare dragons to release back into the wild. Others prefer to test their dragon rearing skills by raising hazardous exotica such as the cockatrice.

COCKATRICE *Gallicus halitosis*

INCREDIBLY dangerous because of the power of its fatal breath, the cockatrice presents an unusual challenge to the home breeder. A mask made of tightly woven silk dipped in a powerful stink-retardant is the very least requirement when dealing with this creature.

A large tame toad will be required in order to help your baby cockatrice to hatch out properly.

No one is sure why a toad is needed to hatch a cockatrice egg, but their slime seems to play a part.

BOGCROW

AMERICAN
Draco americanus tex

THE rare American amphithere is prized by breeders due to the fact that its fur grows in a wide variety of colours. It is the dream of some to produce a 'Stars and Stripes' version.

The shell of Draco americanus tex *gives off a phosphorescent glow that helps a parent to locate it.*

LEATHERJAW

PETITES–
DENTS

These extremely resilient eggs can be dropped from a tremendous height with no ill-effects of any kind.

GARGOUILLE *Draco occidentalis minimus*

HANDY for those who live in one of the new high rise apartment blocks that seem to be springing up, the gargouille will sit happily on a windowsill or balcony for days without moving a muscle, giving every appearance of being part of the building.

13

STARTING OUT.

There are two main ways of rearing dragons: obtaining an orphan chick, or hatching an orphan egg. Never attempt to hatch an egg or rear a chick that is not an orphan—the mother dragon will find you, sooner or later, and unpleasantness may very easily result.

WHERE TO OBTAIN AN EGG OR CHICK.

* The Wild. Not recommended unless you can be quite sure the egg or chick is a genuine orphan who needs your help.

* A Shady Dealer. Not recommended unless you are expert at telling a good egg from a bad. Some sell chicks, then steal them back again.

* The Secret and Ancient Society of Dragonologists. The best way to guarantee quality, but the waiting list is extremely long.

* A Registered Dragon Breeder. Sadly, the scarcity of dragons has driven many breeders out of business.

Beware of offers from shady dealers on Shadwell Dock.

KNOWING A GOOD EGG.

Unlike a curate's egg, a dragon's egg must be entirely good—not just in parts. Test it by seeing if it sinks in boiling water [it will], dissolves in acid [it will not], or by unwrapping it [if you can, it is an Easter egg].

RAISING FROM THE EGG vs ORPHAN ADOPTION.

In general, it is better to raise a chick from the egg. It is easier to form a firm bond with a new-born chick than with one that is sure to be missing its mother.

PREPARING YOUR HOME FOR THE NEW ARRIVAL.

Before introducing a dragon chick into your home, you must make sure that anything really valuable is out of harm's way. Chicks chew, claw and scratch, are quite likely to steal shiny objects to hide, or attempt to set fire to flammable objects. Make sure you have adequate stocks of food. It is also important to set up a 'home base' for the new arrival, so that you can get to know each other safely.

If it is too bothersome to set up a 'lair' indoors...   *...make sure that your garden is fenced in.*

HATCHING FROM AN EGG.

Having obtained your egg, it must be taken home as quickly as possible, in order to keep it warm. Then it must be placed on a nest of live coals, which must be kept burning during the incubation period of 36 months. In the early months it is important to turn the egg each day, so that the yolk inside does not stick to the inner shell.

1. Be Prepared.
European dragon eggs all take 1,095 days to incubate. You can tell when they will hatch, if you know when they were laid.

2. Listen for Knocking.
As soon as the dragon chick is ready to hatch it will begin tapping at the shell with its egg horn.

3. Fetch Hatching Tools.
Useful hatching tools include a sledgehammer to help crack the eggshell, hot water and towels to clean the newborn chick, and tongs to grasp it.

4. Smash Severely.
Help Baby hatch by smashing the shell with a sledgehammer. Do not repeat once Baby is born.

5. Bond With Baby.
Wash the baby with the water, wrap it in a towel, and bond with it. "Coochie-coochie-coo!"

DRAGON CHICK DOS AND DON'TS.

These dos and don'ts apply equally to newly hatched chicks who are, as you will find, rapid developers. Remember: If you can keep your head while everything burns around you, then you're a dragonologist, my son.

DO:

* Refer to yourself as "Mummy" or "Daddy".
* Place some shiny objects in the chick's new "lair".
* Spend time with your new chick each day.
* House-train your new chick as quickly as possible.
* Keep your chick fed.

DON'T:

* Refer to your sister as "Breakfast" or "Dinner".
* Leave iron and flint objects lying around.
* Leave your chick alone for weeks on end.
* Ignore "bad" behaviour— deal with it as it happens.
* Run out of food.

FEEDING AND
FIRST AID.

Most keen dragonologists know that a 40- to 50 acre farm with a head of 300 cows should be just about enough for one chick. However, it is useful to vary the dragon's diet from time to time, to make sure that it gets all of the essential minerals and nutrients that it needs to grow.

RECIPES FOR SUCCESS.

These recipes show how a dragon's favourite snacks can easily be incorporated into its meals. Please avoid including animals such as polar bears and elephants, that require conservation themselves.

FROST DRAGON RECIPE
'POLAR BEAR PIE'

Ingredients:
150 oily fish such as mackerel
10 gallons white sauce
Parsley to garnish
[Never use real *polar bears]*

Place the all of the oily fish in a receptacle such as a 25-gallon cauldron, add white sauce and parsley and freeze solid.

MARSUPIAL RECIPE
'KOALA COBBLER'

Ingredients:
15 plump koalas
24 pairs old leather shoes
2 sacks wholemeal flour
Fat or butter

Sauté the shoes until tender. Rub the fat into the flour. Add the minced koalas to the shoes, top with the flour, and bake.

THE IMPORTANCE OF PHYSICAL EXERCISE.

Some first-timers are shocked to find that dragon chicks are quite energetic and need plenty of physical exercise. Without 'letting off steam' [and smoke, and sometimes gouts of flame, too] the chick's natural exuberance may turn destructive. Should this happen, saying "No!" in a firm voice is unlikely to make much of a difference.

Make sure the chick knows what it is supposed to 'fetch'.

BASIC FIRST AID.

As soon as you note the tell-tale sad looks and general 'droopiness' of a poorly dragon, make sure that you wrap it up warm, and provide it with lots of loving care and attention. A dragonological veterinarian may be called if things worsen rapidly.

19

TRAINING.

Dragons are not particularly easy to train, nor is it recommended to train them excessively, given that they must be released back into the wild as soon as they are old enough. However there are a few things that can be done to make living with your new chick a great deal easier—particularly as regards house training.

Luckily, dragons become house-trained after two or three years.

DR. DRAKE'S DRAGON TRAINING TIPS.

DRAGON MESS.

Adult dragons do not make a mess in their own lairs, but chicks need to develop control. Until they do, cover the whole floor with a good 2ft of paper to soak up the mess.

FIRE-BREATHING.

If you go out and leave your chick at home, it does not burn down your house to punish you, but because it is anxious. Make sure it has lot of toys to incinerate.

REWARDS.

While there is little point to punishments—they will just make the dragon sulky and, in more extreme cases, vengeful —there is plenty of reason to provide a good dragon who is exhibiting desired behaviours with tasty rewards.

OTHER BEHAVIOURS.

As your dragon matures, it will take a different sort of interest in the world about it. For example, at first, a chick may find books interesting, but only from the perspective of how brightly they burn. Do not take it to a library at this stage. After the chick has learned to read, it will no doubt adore books, but by then you are unlikely to be able to find a librarian who will let it in.

LEAPING UP.

While no one minds a baby dragon leaping up at them, a fully grown adult is another matter. Make sure you push the chick away from you firmly, and say "No."

ROARING.

When your dragon roars, praise it for raising the alarm, and offer it a treat. Gradually make sure that it stops roaring for at least a minute before it gets the treat.

If you have a female chick, you may find that she steals ordinary hen's eggs from your kitchen so that she can pretend they are her own. She will not damage them, but when you retrieve them you will find that they are all quite perfectly cooked.

EDUCATIONAL
PLAY.

Like many young animals, dragon chicks learn a number of their adult behaviours through play of various sorts. Mock battles are common, but as dragons have a flame-proof skin and you most likely do not, it is wise to initiate games that are as safe as possible.

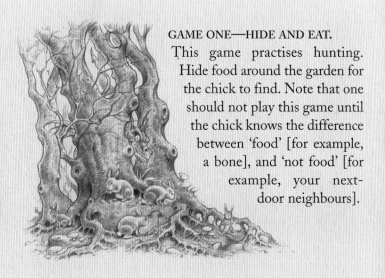

GAME ONE—HIDE AND EAT.
This game practises hunting. Hide food around the garden for the chick to find. Note that one should not play this game until the chick knows the difference between 'food' [for example, a bone], and 'not food' [for example, your next-door neighbours].

Make sure that all of the food is well-hidden.

GAME TWO—LEAP DRAGON.
Dragon siblings often play a game called 'Leap dragon.' As they use their wings to leap over each other, their flight muscles are gently stretched and exercised. It is not a good idea to play this game with older chicks, as they can be too heavy, but it can prove entertaining with younger ones.

A well-fed dragon chick can make the ideal playmate for energetic children.

23

COMMUNICATION.

AN INTRODUCTION TO *DRAGON SIGNING*.

Dear little Torcher makes his very first 'Treasure' sign.

Research suggests dragon chicks can recognise and use simple signs much sooner than they can talk. *Dragon Signing* lets you communicate with a chick long before its vocal chords have developed.

BASIC TECHNIQUE

There are no hard and fast rules about dragon signing, although the signs I suggest here have proved useful. They have been developed so that both dragons and humans find them reasonably easy to make. Simply make sure that the dragon sees you make the appropriate sign at any given time, and it will soon begin to copy you.

Not Food.

Food.

Treasure.

Attack.

Lair.

Good Dragon.

When it is time to move on from Dragon Signing *and learn first words, you may create your own teaching materials, or else choose those available in the* BabyDrake™ *range.*

My First Dragon ABC from *BabyDrake*™.

C is for Claw.

D is for Diamond.

A is for Amulet.

B is for Bone.

E is for Egg.

DRAGON MILESTONES.

After the 'honeymoon period' of the first year, when a properly supervised dragon chick makes a delightful companion, the dragon's wild nature is more and more in evidence until the end of the fifth year when, fully grown, it must finally be released back into the wild.

THE TERRIBLE TWOS.

THE 'Terrible Twos' are so named because the dragon will have grown fairly large, but will not yet have become house-trained. Keep a shovel by the door until the chick learns that certain activities must be done outside.

THE TRAUMATIC THREES.

DURING this stage—which is not at all traumatic for the dragon chick—the dragon first begins to show signs of hoarding behaviour. Shiny objects will be collected from relatives, visitors and neighbours, and defended in an energetic way. Luckily, a three-year-old dragon will not yet be able to produce fire effectively. However, it is still probably safer to wait for a moment when the dragon is distracted—or is fast asleep—before attempting to reclaim any stolen goods.

THE FRUSTRATING FOURS.

THE 'Frustrating Fours' actually are frustrating for the dragon itself. During this period it puts on a growth spurt which tends to make it lose its natural gracefulness. Additionally, it is during the fourth year that most dragons attempt to fly—often with hilarious results. However, it is usually better not to laugh too loudly.

If at first you don't succeed, fly, fly and fly again...

THE FRIGHTFUL FIVES.

IT is a brave dragonologist who is able to endure a full-blown episode of the 'Frightful Fives', when a dragon, still an inexpert flyer, becomes restless. It is at this time that fire is finally produced with ease—a clear sign that the dragon is nearing maturity and must soon leave the 'nest'.

LEAVING HOME.

RELEASING A DRAGON INTO THE WILD.

At last the time comes that all dragonologists dread—when the chicks we have cared for so much grow too large and savage to be looked after at home, and must be released back into the wild. Do not forget that our main aim is the protection and conservation of *wild* dragons.

NEW HOME CHECKLIST.

* Far from human beings.
* Plentiful food supply.
* No other dragons nearby.
* Large enough area.
* Possible lair sites nearby.
* Not too hard to visit.
* The right habitat for the dragon you are releasing.

It is important to be firm when releasing a dragon into the wild. At first it may not understand why it has to go.

After only a few hours you will find that the dragon is completely at home in its new environment.

APPENDIX I.

DRAGON LULLABIES

Sometimes dragon chicks find it difficult to settle into a new home. On such occasions traditional lullabies may prove useful. Remember that the chick may well not understand the words you use, so much as the tone of your voice, which must be as loud and deep as possible.

HUSH LITTLE WYVERN

Hush, Little Wyvern,
Don't say a word,
Mama's gonna find you
An elephant herd.
If those elephants
Are eaten by spring,
Momma's gonna find you
A diamond ring.

ROUND AND ROUND THE CASTLE

Round and round the castle
Like an amphithere,
A-one puff, a-two puff,
We'll burn it down from here.

Round and round the castle,
Like an angry wyrm,
We'll give a roar,
And then some more,
And watch the people squirm!

ROCK-A-BYE DRAGON

Rock-a-bye Dragon
On the hill top,
A knight will ride by
But then he will stop.

When that knight stops
The dragon will roar.
The knight will not ever
Go there any more.

ITSY-BITSY DRAGON

Itsy-bitsy dragon
Climbed up the magma spout,
Up came an eruption
And blew the dragon out.
Down came the lava
Just like a shower of rain,
Then Itsy-bitsy dragon
Climbed down the spout again.

THREE BLIND KNIGHTS

Three blind knights.
Three blind knights.
See how they run!
See how they run!
They all ran after the
Knucker chick,
Who gave each one a
venomous lick,
Did you ever hear of a sillier
trick than three blind knights?

TWINKLE, TWINKLE

Twinkle, twinkle, little star,
How I wonder what you are,
Up above the world so high,
Like a diamond in the sky.
Could I fetch you if I soared?
And bring you back to swell
my hoard?

WEE WILLIE WYVERN

Wee Willie Wyvern
Flies through the town.
Huffing and puffing,
He's going to burn it down.
Scratching at the window,
Clawing at the lock,
"Are the children in their beds?
They're going to get a shock!"

APPENDIX II.
A DRAGON RECORD BOOK.

Every dragonologist loves to record those extra-special moments in their chick's life for posterity. Below you can see a sample of such a record—on the next page there is a blank version that you may copy to use yourself.

NAME:	Torcher
DRAGON TYPE:	European
AGE:	2 years
WEIGHT AT BIRTH:	15 lbs
LENGTH AT BIRTH:	1 ft 8 inches

FAVOURITE FOOD:	The whole hog
FAVOURITE TOY:	My flame-proof cloak
FIRST STEPS:	2 hours old
FIRST SIGNS OF HOARDING BEHAVIOUR:	At 2 hours 2 minutes old, he stole my pocket-watch. Is this a record?
FIRST WORDS:	"Eat" "Boy" "Treasure"
FIRST FLAME:	2 hours 3 minutes old

OTHER NOTES: Torcher is a very inquisitive little fellow, but he rather lost his spark the day he fell poorly. Luckily, he was soon up and about again after a dose of my specially-formulated linctus. It is amazing how he seems to know when it is Sunday lunchtime. You've got to watch him like a hawk in the kitchen!

MY DRAGON RECORD BOOK.

This record book has been produced by the S.A.S.D for Dr. Ernest Drake, and comes from his book *Bringing Up Baby Dragons*. Start your record by making a sketch of your own dragon in the box below.

NAME:

DRAGON TYPE:

AGE:

WEIGHT AT BIRTH:

LENGTH AT BIRTH:

FAVOURITE FOOD:

FAVOURITE TOY:

FIRST STEPS:

FIRST SIGNS OF
HOARDING BEHAVIOUR:

FIRST WORDS:

FIRST FLAME:

OTHER NOTES:

AFTERWORD.

Remember that the study of dragons—always with a view to their conservation and protection—can be the start of a lifetime of scientific adventures. If you need more information, I suggest you read my other books *Dragonology* and *Working with Dragons*, which are both available to members of the *Secret and Ancient Society of Dragonologists*.

Ernest Drake